MW01283777

VIRGINIA

BY MOIRA ROSE DONOHUE

CONTENT CONSULTANT
Peter Wallenstein, PhD
Professor of History
Virginia Polytechnic Institute and State University

Core Library

An Imprint of Abdo Publishing
abdobooks.com

abdobooks.com

Published by Abdo Publishing, a division of ABDO, PO Box 398166, Minneapolis, Minnesota 55439. Copyright © 2023 by Abdo Consulting Group, Inc. International copyrights reserved in all countries. No part of this book may be reproduced in any form without written permission from the publisher. Core Library™ is a trademark and logo of Abdo Publishing.

Printed in the United States of America, North Mankato, Minnesota.
052022
092022

Cover Photos: Shutterstock Images, map, icons; Shane Sabin/Shutterstock Images, deer
Interior Photos: Matt McClain/Shutterstock Images, 4–5, 43; Red Line Editorial, 7 (Virginia), 7 (USA); Joseph Sohm/Shutterstock Images, 10–11; Shutterstock Images, 15; Lukasz Stefanski/Shutterstock Images, 17 (flag); Ernie Decker/iStockphoto, 17 (bird); Mary Swift/Shutterstock Images, 17 (dog); iStockphoto, 17 (flower), 26, 45; OG Photo/iStockphoto, 17 (butterfly); Bettmann/Getty Images, 19; Kristi Blokhin/Shutterstock Images, 22–23; John M. Chase/iStockphoto, 30–31; Bill Clark/CQ Roll Call/AP Images, 34–35; Julian C. Wilson/AP Images, 36–37; Steve Helber/AP Images, 38

Editor: Marie Pearson
Series Designer: Joshua Olson

Library of Congress Control Number: 2021951550

Publisher's Cataloging-in-Publication Data

Names: Donohue, Moira Rose, author.
Title: Virginia / by Moira Rose Donohue
Description: Minneapolis, Minnesota : Abdo Publishing, 2023 | Series: Core library of US states | Includes online resources and index.
Identifiers: ISBN 9781532197888 (lib. bdg.) | ISBN 9781098270643 (ebook)
Subjects: LCSH: U.S. states--Juvenile literature. | Southeastern States--Juvenile literature. | Virginia--History--Juvenile literature. | Physical geography--United States--Juvenile literature.
Classification: DDC 975.5--dc23

Population demographics broken down by race and ethnicity come from the 2019 census estimate. Population totals come from the 2020 census.

CONTENTS

THE OLD DOMINION

A man wearing stockings and large-buckled shoes removes his three-cornered hat. He opens a door and bows to visitors. Beyond the door is a marble-floored entrance hall. It's decorated with swords and muskets. This is not a time machine. It's a tour of the Governor's Palace in Colonial Williamsburg, Virginia.

Colonial Williamsburg is a living museum of Virginia as it was before the Revolutionary War (1775–1783). People dress in colonial clothes and use colonial manners and speech.

Visitors to Colonial Williamsburg can enjoy carriage rides past the Governor's Palace.

HIGH TIDES

The East Coast is often battered by hurricanes. Virginia's shore curves inward from the ocean. That helps it avoid many storms that strike states farther south. But some storms still hit the state. George Washington's home, Mount Vernon, is on the east side of the state. He wrote about a hurricane that blew in on July 23, 1788. He said, "About Noon the Wind suddenly shifted from No. Et. [Northeast] to So. Wt. [Southwest] and blew the remaining part of the day as violently from that quarter. The tide about this time rose near or quite 4 feet [1.2 m] higher than it was ever known to do."

Visitors can stop by the weavers' shop. Women there sit at spinning wheels turning wool into yarn. Two blocks away, blacksmiths are hammering. With strong blows, they shape scalding bars of iron into tools.

ABOUT VIRGINIA

Virginia is part of the US region called the South. The state is located in about the middle of the East Coast. Maryland and the US capital of Washington, DC,

MAP OF
VIRGINIA

Early colonists were given orders to explore the James River. Trace its path backward from the Atlantic Ocean. What major city does it lead to?

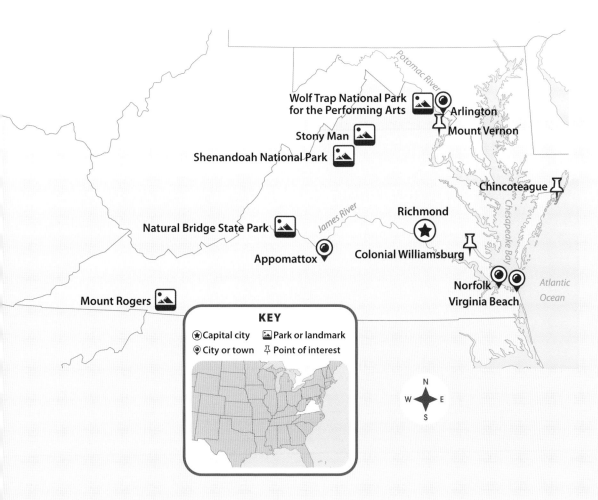

Potomac River

Wolf Trap National Park
for the Performing Arts

Arlington

Mount Vernon

Stony Man

Shenandoah National Park

Chincoteague

Natural Bridge State Park

James River

Richmond

Chesapeake Bay

Appomattox

Colonial Williamsburg

Mount Rogers

Norfolk

Virginia Beach

Atlantic
Ocean

KEY

⭐ Capital city 🏞 Park or landmark

◉ City or town ⚓ Point of interest

N
W E
S

border it to the north. Tennessee and North Carolina are to the south. On the west side, Virginia touches Kentucky and West Virginia. Eastern Virginia ends at the Chesapeake Bay and the Atlantic Ocean.

Virginia has mountains, beaches, and rolling hills. Virginia's location gives it a mild climate. While people in the state enjoy all four seasons, it's rarely too cold or too hot.

MOTHER OF PRESIDENTS

One of Virginia's nicknames is the Mother of Presidents. Eight US presidents were born there, more than in any other state. These presidents were George Washington, Thomas Jefferson, James Madison, James Monroe, William Henry Harrison, John Tyler, Zachary Taylor, and Woodrow Wilson.

More than 8.6 million people live in Virginia. The main cities and communities are Virginia Beach, Norfolk, Chesapeake, Arlington, and the capital city of Richmond. The largest city is Virginia Beach. But approximately one-third of the people reside in the northern part of the state, near DC. Many Virginians work in the service industry. They have jobs in health care and education. Other key industries in Virginia are technology, farming, lumber, and fishing.

Virginia's nickname is the Old Dominion. The word *dominion* means "an area of land controlled by a government." The nickname refers to the fact that Virginia was England's first colony in North America. Virginia has a long history. It played an important part in the history of the United States. And it continues to help shape the nation today.

EXPLORE ONLINE

Chapter One discusses Colonial Williamsburg. The website below has a map of Colonial Williamsburg. Look closely and find the Governor's Palace. Does the map answer any questions you had about Colonial Williamsburg?

MAP OF COLONIAL WILLIAMSBURG

abdocorelibrary.com/virginia

HISTORY OF VIRGINIA

People first lived in what is now Virginia more than 10,000 years ago. By the 1500s CE, Iroquoian, Siouan, and Algonquian-speaking peoples lived there. These included the Powhatans. People lived in villages and towns. They grew crops such as beans and squash. Nations formed alliances.

JAMESTOWN

The first Europeans visited the Virginia area in the 1500s. But they did not stay. Eventually England wanted to set up a colony in Virginia. In 1607 three ships brought more than

A statue of Pocahontas, one of the most famous Powhatans, stands at the site of Jamestown today.

11

100 English colonists across the Atlantic Ocean. Captain Christopher Newport directed the ships up the James River. He anchored the ships outside the area now known as Jamestown.

The colonists struggled to survive at first. Some died of diseases. At the time, a man named Wahunsunacock was the paramount chief of the Powhatans. He sent food to help the colonists. In 1609 a drought caused food to become scarce. The colonists began fighting with the American Indians for supplies. One winter most of the colonists died.

HAPPY THANKSGIVING

Most people think the first Thanksgiving was in Plymouth, Massachusetts. But there were thanksgiving meals in what is now the United States before that famous one. On December 4, 1619, settlers at Berkeley Plantation, Virginia, gave thanks and prayers. They shared a meal, eating most likely oysters and ham. This was almost two years before the Thanksgiving in Plymouth.

Tensions grew between the Powhatans and the colonists. The colonists sometimes became violent. This led to war. The First Anglo-Powhatan War happened from 1609 to 1614. In 1610 ships arrived from England carrying more food and new colonists. The settlement at Jamestown grew. It was England's first permanent settlement in North America.

War continued. Eventually colonists captured Wahunsunacock's daughter Pocahontas. English colonist John Rolfe married her. The fighting ended for a while. Rolfe and Pocahontas traveled to England in 1616. She died the next year before she could return to Virginia.

Meanwhile the settlers took more and more land from the Powhatans. The Powhatan people grew angry. They fought with the colonists in 1622. The colonists defeated the Powhatans. A third war broke out in 1644. This was the final war. The English won. The surviving Powhatans stayed in Virginia, but under British rule.

GIVE ME LIBERTY

Virginia and the other English colonies expanded and thrived. Soon they wanted representation in the British government. But England would not give them the representation they wanted. A Virginian named Patrick Henry begged the colonies to seek independence from the British. He gave stirring speeches, including one at Saint John's Church in Richmond in 1775.

Virginia played a big role in the Revolutionary War. In 1776 the colonies

Thomas Jefferson, *right*, has been depicted in many pieces of art about the creation of the Declaration of Independence.

declared their separation from England. Thomas Jefferson of Virginia wrote the Declaration of Independence. Virginian farmer George Washington led the Continental Army. After years of fighting, the colonial army beat the British at the Battle of Yorktown in southeastern Virginia. Then the colonies won their independence. Washington and James Madison helped form the new country of the United States. Virginia became the tenth state on July 25, 1788. Its state government is made up of the legislative, executive, and judicial branches. These branches write laws, approve them, and apply them in court cases.

CIVIL WAR

In the 1860s another war broke out. This time it was over slavery. As far back as 1619, Black people from Africa were kidnapped and brought to Virginia. They were enslaved and forced to work on large farms called plantations. Many white Virginians, including Thomas Jefferson, George Washington, and Patrick Henry, were slaveholders.

More and more, white people disagreed about slavery. Plantations that relied on slave labor were common in the South. But most people in northern states did not want new territories in the West to allow slavery. Many wanted slavery to end. In 1861 Virginia and ten other states seceded from, or left, the United States and formed the Confederacy, where slavery could continue. The Civil War (1861–1865) began.

VIRGINIA
QUICK FACTS

There is a lot that makes Virginia special. How do these facts and symbols help you understand the many points of pride for people in the state?

Abbreviation: VA
Nickname: The Old Dominion
Motto: *Sic semper tyrannis* (Thus always to tyrants)
Date of statehood: July 25, 1788
Capital: Richmond
Population: 8,631,393
Area: 42,775 square miles (110,787 sq km)

STATE SYMBOLS

State bird
Northern cardinal

State flower
American dogwood

State dog
American foxhound

State insect
Tiger swallowtail butterfly

General Robert E. Lee of Virginia led the Confederate Army. Richmond became the capital of the Confederacy. Several important battles were fought in Virginia, including two battles near Manassas and one in Petersburg. In 1865 Lee and the Confederate Army surrendered to the Union at the courthouse in Appomattox.

CIVIL RIGHTS

The Civil War ended slavery. But it did not end discrimination in Virginia. Instead Virginia's government passed Jim Crow laws. Under these laws, people of color had to stay separate from white people. For example, Black children could not go to the same schools as white children. Schools for Black students did not receive as much money as schools for white students. Black schools often didn't have enough room. Students attended classes in temporary structures.

In 1951 Virginia high school student Barbara Johns wanted to do something about Jim Crow laws. She and

Oliver Hill, *right*, received the Presidential Medal of Freedom in 1999 for his civil rights work.

other Black students went on strike. They held signs at their school to protest the unequal conditions. Oliver Hill, a famous civil rights lawyer in Virginia, filed a lawsuit for Johns. The case was combined with several others and became known as *Brown v. Board of Education*. The Supreme Court of the United States heard the case. In 1954 the Supreme Court decided that segregation in public schools must end.

But in Virginia, many white people fought desegregation. Parents often sent children to private schools. Finally the Supreme Court ordered public schools to desegregate right away.

RECENT VIRGINIA HISTORY

Virginia has seen signs of progress. In 1989 Virginia voted to make Douglas Wilder the first elected Black governor in the United States. But racism continues. In 2017 a group that included white supremacists gathered for a rally in Charlottesville. The group was protesting the proposed removal of Confederate monuments. Clashes with police and counterprotesters led to violence. The city still removed the statues. It agreed with arguments that they promoted racism.

The Pentagon in Arlington is the headquarters for the US Department of Defense. On September 11, 2001, terrorists crashed a plane into the building. More than 180 people died. The building has been repaired. But the tragedy affected the nation. As Virginia continues to encounter struggles and triumphs, its rich history continues to progress.

STRAIGHT TO THE
SOURCE

Barbara Johns made a plan to challenge the conditions in her all-Black high school, Robert Russa Moton. Johns explained her plan:

> *We would make signs and I would give a speech stating our dissatisfaction and we would march out [of] the school and people would hear us and see us and understand our difficulty and would sympathize with our plight and would grant us our new school building and our teachers would be proud and the students would learn more and it would be grand.*

Source: "Biography: Barbara Rose Johns Powell." *Robert Russa Moton Museum*, n.d., motonmuseum.org. Accessed 30 June 2021.

CONSIDER YOUR AUDIENCE

Adapt this passage for a different audience, such as your younger friends. Write a blog post conveying this same information for the new audience. How does your post differ from the original text and why?

GEOGRAPHY AND CLIMATE

Virginia's geography is diverse. The state has five regions that each run mostly north to south. The east side of the state is a coastal plain called the Tidewater region. The land is flat and swampy. It runs along the Chesapeake Bay and Atlantic Ocean. The area was created by east-flowing rivers and the melting of glaciers thousands of years ago.

The Piedmont region borders it to the west. The Piedmont is the largest land region in Virginia. Its name comes from a French

Virginia has many rolling hills.

word meaning "foot of the mountains." It is separated from the Tidewater region by a fall line. This is a line along which rivers drop, forming waterfalls and rapids on their way to the ocean. Rolling hills characterize the Piedmont area. Farther west the hills get taller. This is the Blue Ridge region. The rounded mountains there formed millions of years ago. They are part of the Appalachian Mountains. From a distance, the mountains appear blue because of certain chemicals released by the forests there. This creates a hazy effect. One mountain peak called Stony Man looks like the face of a bearded man. Mount Rogers is the highest peak in the state at 5,729 feet (1,746 m) above sea level.

Beyond the Blue Ridge is the Valley and Ridge region. This region is home to many limestone caves and caverns. It also includes the Shenandoah Valley. Tucked between mountains, the soil in the flatter Shenandoah Valley is good for farming. The fifth region is the Appalachian Plateau, a small area in the far west. A number of farms grow Christmas trees there.

Virginia has four major rivers that spill into the Chesapeake Bay. They are the Potomac, the Rappahannock, the York, and the James. Early settlers sailed inland along these rivers. But eventually they hit the fall line. Their ships couldn't easily travel farther west because of the waterfalls there. This is why the cities of Petersburg, Richmond, and Fredericksburg are located along the fall line.

MUSICAL MINERALS

The movement of rocks that created Virginia also created many underground caves and caverns. These include Luray Caverns. It's in the northern part of the state. Luray Caverns formed over millions of years as water dripped down or seeped up through the limestone rocks. The drying water left behind calcite. Some calcite deposits form in columns from the ceiling called stalactites. Visitors can sometimes hear eerie music there. It's from the Great Stalacpipe Organ. A musician can press keys on the organ. The keys cause rubber mallets to tap certain stalactites, making sound.

The city of Richmond lies on the James River. The river is rocky there.

GOLDILOCKS CLIMATE

Some say Virginia has a Goldilocks climate. The weather there is not too cold and not too hot—it's just right. The average yearly rainfall for the state, 44 inches (112 cm), is just above the national average. The Tidewater is the warmest region. The summers on the east coast are warm and humid. The winters feel mild. It's chillier west of the Blue Ridge. Winter temperatures there run at least 5 degrees Fahrenheit (2.8°C) colder. While the average yearly snowfall for the state is 14 inches (36 cm), the western regions get more snow.

The Virginia coast along the Atlantic Ocean curves inward from North Carolina. Because of its location, major hurricanes that hit the East Coast often miss Virginia. But in colonial days, it was battered by several hurricanes. Virginia also suffered damage from Hurricane Camille in 1969 and Hurricane Isabel in 2003.

PLANTS AND ANIMALS

Virginia has many trees. Oak, walnut, and elm trees grow there. So does the flowering dogwood tree, the state flower and tree. This tree is a favorite of the northern cardinal, the state bird. Today almost two-thirds of Virginia is forested. Other common trees in Virginia are loblolly pines, tulip poplars, and maples. Purple swamp milkweed and coral honeysuckle are some of the flowering plants native to Virginia.

PERSPECTIVES

STATE SALAMANDER

In 2018 the state legislature of Virginia voted to name the red salamander as the Virginia state salamander. Several years earlier, three children in Fairfax watched as a lake was dredged. They saw salamanders scurry about as their habitat was disturbed. The students promoted awareness of these animals. They worked to make the red salamander the Virginia state salamander. One of the children, Jonah Kim, said, "We chose the red salamander because it lives throughout Virginia. . . . We thought it was easily recognizable and would be interesting to people who have never seen a salamander."

The state insect, the tiger swallowtail butterfly, flutters in milkweeds or honeysuckle. Early European settlers in Virginia found white-tailed deer, wild turkeys, and oysters. These animals still live in the state. Other animals in Virginia today include squirrels, bats, rabbits, and black bears.

STRAIGHT TO THE
SOURCE

Native plants are those that have developed in a particular region. The Virginia Department of Conservation and Recreation recommends that people plant native plants:

> Plants evolve . . . in response to physical . . . processes characteristic of a region: the climate, soils, timing of rainfall, drought, and frost; and interactions with the other species inhabiting the local community. Thus native plants possess certain traits that make them uniquely adapted to local conditions, providing a practical and ecologically valuable alternative for landscaping, conservation and restoration projects, and as livestock forage. In addition, native plants . . . often [surpass] non-natives in ruggedness and resistance to drought, insects and disease.

Source: "What Are Native Plants?" *Virginia DCR*, n.d., dcr.virginia.gov. Accessed 30 June 2021.

BACK IT UP

The author of this passage is using evidence to support a point. Write a paragraph describing the point the author is making. Then write down two or three pieces of evidence the author uses to make the point.

CHAPTER FOUR

RESOURCES AND ECONOMY

The Algonquian-speaking peoples farmed corn, beans, and squash. Colonists learned to grow these crops too. They also planted tobacco and other crops to sell. They enslaved American Indians and people from Africa to make growing crops more profitable.

Because of Virginia's fertile land, agriculture remains an important industry in the state. It has more than 43,000 farms. The main crops include soybeans, corn, flowers,

Some people in Virginia go crabbing in the Chesapeake Bay. They use traps with bait inside to catch crabs.

PERSPECTIVES

BIG FISH

The striped bass, sometimes called the rockfish, is found in saltwater areas in Virginia. It can grow to be 5 feet (1.5 m) long. It is caught commercially and sold for food. But amateur anglers like to catch this fish as well. Recently the Virginia Marine Resources Commission found that the striped bass was being overfished. To protect this resource, the commission voted to limit the size and number of fish that recreational fishers could catch and keep. The commission hopes to protect large females so that they can continue to produce new fish.

hay, and tobacco. Virginia farmers also raise broiler chickens, cattle, and pigs. Commercial fishing is a large industry along the Atlantic coast. Some of the aquatic animals caught are striped bass, trout, oysters, and blue crabs.

The lumber industry is the third-largest industry in the state. More than 15.3 million acres (6.2 million ha) in Virginia are used for growing timber. Hardwood tree products are used in the state and also exported.

Because trees are being replanted, lumber is a renewable resource.

Virginia is home to a variety of rocks and minerals. Coal is mined in some parts of the state. It is used for fuel. Virginia also has some valuable mineral deposits. Gold has been found in the Piedmont and Blue Ridge regions.

SOLDIERS, SAILORS, AND TOURISTS

Virginia is home to many military bases, including the Naval Station Norfolk and the Marine Corps Base Quantico. These bases provide many jobs for military workers. One industry related to the military is shipbuilding. The American Indians and the early settlers built canoes

I SPY

Hidden behind trees and a guarded gate in Langley, near Arlington, is the Central Intelligence Agency (CIA). The CIA is part of the United States government. CIA agents collect secret information about foreign countries. Other workers analyze the information to help protect US citizens.

The Pentagon is one of many federal government workplaces in Virginia.

and sailing ships. Today Virginians in Newport News build aircraft carriers and submarines for the military. In addition, more than 27,000 people work at the Pentagon. Many other Virginians also work for the federal government. Some work in Washington, DC, but live in Virginia.

Tourism makes up an important part of Virginia's economy. It offers jobs in the hospitality industry, such as those at hotels and restaurants. Millions of people visit Virginia Beach and Virginia's many historic sites every year. Other key industries include technology, engineering, and service industries such as banking and health care.

PEOPLE
AND PLACES

Many famous people have come from Virginia. Bill "Bojangles" Robinson, the father of modern tap dance, was born in Richmond. In 1968 Arthur Ashe from Richmond became the first person to win the US Open tennis tournament. Singer and songwriter Pharrell Williams and actress Wanda Sykes are also from Virginia.

About 61 percent of the people living in Virginia today are white. Approximately 20 percent are Black, and 10 percent are Hispanic or Latino. Approximately 7 percent

Arthur Ashe was still only an amateur player when he was playing tennis tournaments in 1968.

American Indians in Virginia, including those of the Upper Mattaponi Tribe, work with the state government to protect their peoples' interests.

are Asian. Although a large number of American Indians lived in Virginia when the settlers arrived, many were killed in the wars with the settlers. In addition, many more died of diseases the settlers brought to the area. About 30,000 people in the state today are American Indian. There are seven federally recognized tribes. People of other races and ethnicities make up the rest of the population.

UNFORGETTABLE PLACES

There are many places for tourists to visit. People can visit museums on the Mattaponi Indian Reservation and the Pamunkey Reservation. The museums include information on the history of the peoples and their lives today. Colonial Williamsburg and George Washington's home, Mount Vernon, are popular sites. Near Charlottesville people can visit Monticello, Thomas Jefferson's home. He designed it himself. Those interested in the Civil War can tour the battlefield at Manassas.

In northern Virginia, visitors can find Arlington National Cemetery. More than 400,000 service

PERSPECTIVES

NICKELS TO DOLLARS

Maggie L. Walker of Richmond was the daughter of a formerly enslaved person. Walker was the first Black American woman to start a bank. She established the Saint Luke Penny Savings Bank in 1903 so Black people could have access to loans and savings accounts. She said, "Let us have a bank that will take the nickels and turn them into dollars." During her lifetime, she worked for better conditions for Black people. She continued her efforts even as her health declined. Today her house in Richmond is a national historic site.

AND THEY'RE OFF!

The Chincoteague ponies aren't the only famous horses in Virginia. Secretariat was a Thoroughbred racehorse. He was born in Caroline County. In 1973 he won all three races in the Triple Crown. He set the record for the fastest time in each of the races. By 2021 no other single horse had broken those records.

members are buried there. It's also home to President John F. Kennedy's grave and the Tomb of the Unknown Soldier. Some soldiers who died in battle and could not be identified were buried at this tomb.

Virginia has many state and national parks. One is Shenandoah National Park. In Shenandoah visitors can drive along the Skyline Drive atop the Blue Ridge Mountains. They can hike more than 500 miles (800 km) of trails there. Hikers can find streams, birds, rock formations, and black bears. For more natural beauty, visitors can travel south to delight in the sights at Natural Bridge State Park. Natural Bridge is a rock arch made of limestone. Cedar Creek carved it out over many years. For live performances, people flock to the outdoor theater at Wolf Trap National Park for the Performing Arts. And for fun, many tourists travel to Virginia Beach and the island of Chincoteague. At Chincoteague they can watch the annual pony swim. Wild ponies on a neighboring island are rounded up and herded to swim across a narrow channel to be auctioned off. This helps keep the ponies from overpopulating the island. From history to natural beauty, Virginia is full of adventures.

FURTHER EVIDENCE

Chapter Five discusses tourism in Virginia. What is the main point of this chapter? What evidence does the author provide to support this point? Go to the article at the website below. Is there evidence that supports this main point?

VIRGINIA

abdocorelibrary.com/virginia

IMPORTANT DATES

10,000 years ago
Humans are present in what is now Virginia.

1607
English colonists set up Jamestown, the first permanent English colony in what would become the United States. The Powhatan people help them survive.

1640s
After decades of fighting, the English colonists defeat the Powhatan people. The Powhatan people come under British rule.

1776
The Declaration of Independence, drafted by Virginian Thomas Jefferson, declares the colonies free from British rule.

1788
Virginia becomes the tenth state on July 25.

1861–1865

Virginia and ten other Southern states secede from the Union and form the Confederacy to fight during the Civil War. The Confederacy surrenders at Appomattox, and the Civil War ends.

1951

Barbara Johns and her fellow students go on strike for better school conditions. This case and others lead to the end of school segregation.

2001

Terrorists attack the Pentagon, leaving more than 180 people dead.

STOP AND
THINK

You Are There

Chapter One of this book discusses visiting Colonial Williamsburg. Imagine you are on a tour of this historical site. Write a letter home telling your family what you learned about how people lived at the time. What sorts of jobs did people have? What clothes did they wear?

Tell the Tale

Chapter Five mentions Shenandoah National Park in Virginia. Imagine you're hiking through the park. What region of Virginia would you be in? What animals might you see? Which ones might you stay away from? Describe your visit in 200 words.

Take a Stand

Chapter Three discusses Virginia's many geographic regions. Which one do you think sounds most beautiful and why?

Why Do I Care?

Chapter Four talks about some of the natural resources in Virginia. Think about the resources mentioned. How do these different natural resources affect your life? How would your life change if they weren't available?

GLOSSARY

colony
an area of land that is separate from but controlled by another country

economy
a place's system of goods, services, money, and jobs

hospitality industry
the business of receiving and serving guests, as in a hotel

paramount
most important; highest

plantation
a large farm where the workers live on-site

plateau
high, flat land

segregation
the separation of groups of people based on race, class, or ethnicity

stalactite
an icicle-shaped mineral deposit hanging from the roof of a cave

strike
to refuse to go to work or school until certain demands are met

ONLINE RESOURCES

To learn more about Virginia, visit our free resource websites below.

Visit **abdocorelibrary.com** or scan this QR code for free Common Core resources for teachers and students, including vetted activities, multimedia, and booklinks, for deeper subject comprehension.

Visit **abdobooklinks.com** or scan this QR code for free additional online weblinks for further learning. These links are routinely monitored and updated to provide the most current information available.

LEARN MORE

Elston, Heidi M. D. *Thomas Jefferson*. Abdo, 2021.

Krull, Kathleen. *A Kid's Guide to the American Revolution*. HarperCollins, 2018.

INDEX

About the Author

Although currently residing in Saint Petersburg, Florida, Moira Rose Donohue lived most of her adult life in Virginia. She has authored more than 35 books for children, including several biographies about Virginians such as Maggie L. Walker, Doug Wilder, Arthur Ashe, and Oliver Hill.